WITH

CIRCLES

By Eiji Orii and Masako Orii   Pictures by Kaoru Fujishima

Gareth Stevens Children's Books
Milwaukee

For a free color catalog describing Gareth Stevens' list of high-quality children's books, call 1-800-341-3569 (USA) or 1-800-461-9120 (Canada).

Simple Science Experiments with . . .

Circles	*Ping-Pong Balls*
Light	*Starting and Stopping*
Marbles	*Straws*
Optical Illusions	*Water*

Library of Congress Cataloging-in-Publication Data

Orii, Eiji, 1909-
      Simple science experiments with circles / Eiji Orii and Masako Orii;
Kaoru Fujishima (ill.). — North American ed.
          p. cm. — (Simple science experiments)
      Translated from the Japanese.
      Includes index.
      Summary: Presents experiments demonstrating properties of circles
and loops made of cloth, paper, and string.
      ISBN 1-55532-857-1 (lib. bdg.)
      1. Circle—Experiments—Juvenile literature. 2. Topology
--Experiments—Juvenile literature. [1. Circle—Experiments.
2. Experiments.] I. Orii, Masako. II. Fujishima, Kaoru, ill.
III. Title. IV. Series.
QA484.075   1989
507'.8—dc19   88-23295

North American edition first published in 1989 by

Gareth Stevens Children's Books
1555 North RiverCenter Drive, Suite 201
Milwaukee, Wisconsin 53212, USA

Series editor and additional text: Rita Reitci
Research editor: Scott Enk
Additional illustrations: John Stroh
Design: Laurie Shock

Technical consultant: Jonathan Knopp, Chair, Science Department, Rufus King High School, Milwaukee

Printed in the United States of America

4 5 6 7 8 9 96 95 94 93 92 91

Look at a plain circle. It seems to be a simple thing, doesn't it? But a simple circle can hide a lot of tricks! The rings, loops, and circles you'll read about in this book will help you learn more about patterns and shapes and some of the unexpected things they can do.

Cut a hole in a postcard. Now try
pulling the circle over your body.

It's impossible! Or is it?

Try it this way.

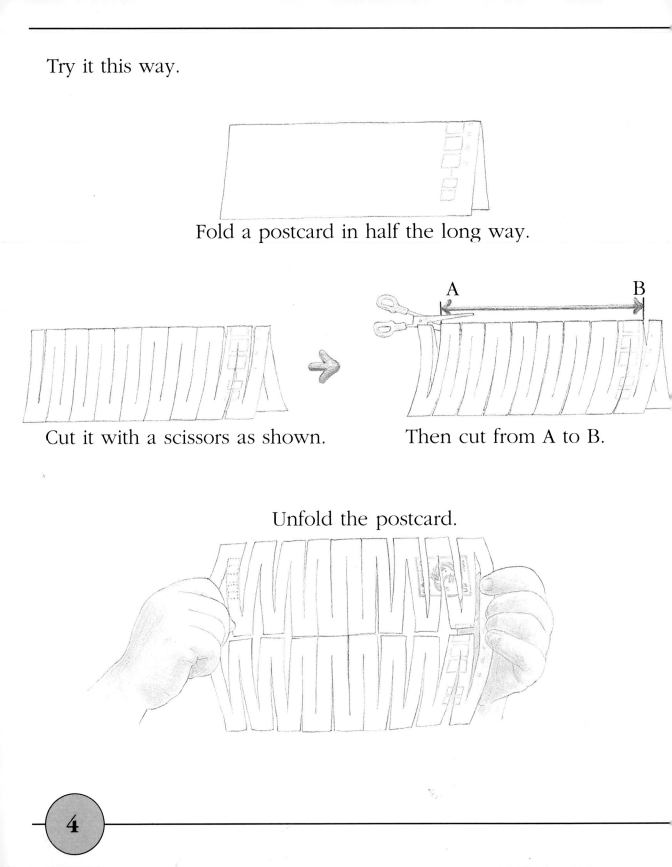

Fold a postcard in half the long way.

Cut it with a scissors as shown.

Then cut from A to B.

Unfold the postcard.

Now you can pull it down over yourself.

Get a piece of paper the same size as a business card. Fold it and cut it the way you cut the postcard. Now pull it over your head.

If you want a bigger loop, do you make your cuts closer together or farther apart? Use two pieces of paper the same size. Make the cuts on one very close together. Make the cuts on the other farther apart.

Put a penny on a piece of paper. Draw a line around the penny. Cut a hole in the paper, following the line of the circle you drew. Can you pass a quarter through the hole without tearing the paper?

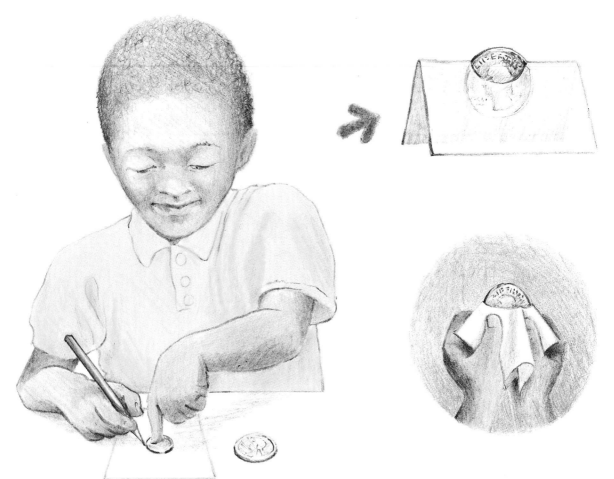

(Hint: Bend the paper very gently to ease the quarter through.)

The cut you made in the paper is big enough to fit over the quarter if you straighten the cut out first.

Try linking strips of cloth.

Cut four pieces of soft cloth. Make each piece 2 inches (5 cm) wide and 6 inches (15 cm) long.

Fold them together as shown. Make holes in the centers as shown by the dots below. Ask an adult to help you make the holes.

What will happen if you take the end of the cloth and pull it through the holes?

The pieces will be linked together!

Get a long piece of string, double it, and loop it through the handle of a cup. Hang the cup by the string on a rod or stick. Can you get the cup loose without untying or cutting the string?

Here's how.

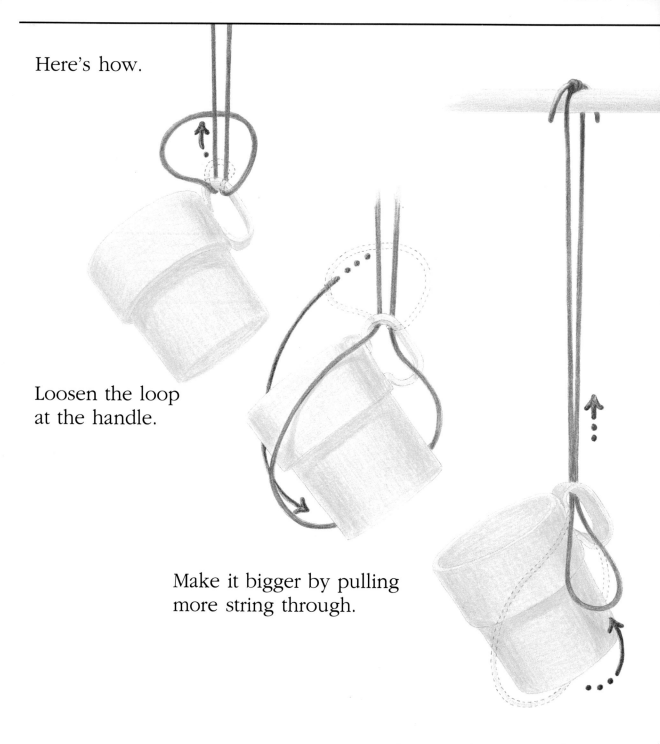

Loosen the loop
at the handle.

Make it bigger by pulling
more string through.

When it's big enough, put
the cup through the loop.

Make a circle with your thumb and index
finger. Have a friend try to break the circle.
This will be easy if your friend pulls your
circle apart with his or her index fingers.

But you can do it
so that the circle
will not break.

This time, when you make a circle with your index finger and thumb, hold your other fingers back stiffly at eye level. Now ask your friend to try to break your circle with his or her index fingers.

Holding the other fingers out stiffly tightens the muscles in your hand. This helps clamp your index finger strongly against your thumb.

Tie a piece of thread into a circle. Fill a dish with water and lay the thread on the surface so that it floats. Does the thread form a perfect circle?

The surface of water tightens up to form a thin, firm "skin" that we call surface tension. The thread is held up on top by the surface tension of the water in the dish.

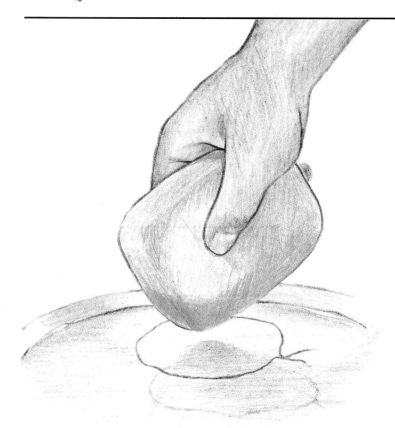

Touch the surface of the water inside the thread with a wet bar of soap. What happens?

Soap weakens the surface tension of water. The water relaxes suddenly in all directions, pulling the thread out into a perfect circle.

Try this using containers of different shapes.

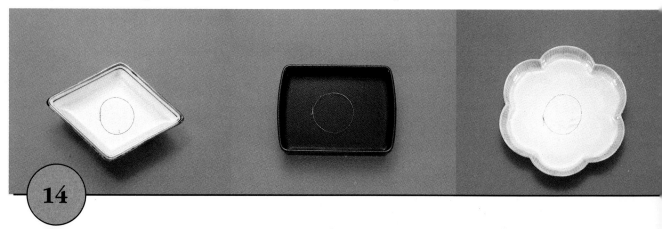

Make shapes from
apple skins.

Ask an adult to skin an apple in
one long unbroken strip.
What kind of shape will you
get if you put the skin on a table?

You will get this!

A loop-the-loop roller
coaster will keep going
as long as you are on it.

Try your own tricks with loops.

Cut a long piece of paper 1 1/2 inches (4 cm) wide. Tape both ends together to make a loop. Keep the strip straight when you do this.

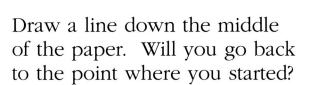

Draw a line down the middle of the paper. Will you go back to the point where you started?

Carefully cut along the line. What happens?

You will get two loops of paper.

Make a different kind of loop.

Cut another long strip of paper. But this time, twist the strip once before you tape the ends to make a loop.

Draw a line down the middle of the paper. What happens when you try to draw it back to the starting point? How many sides does this strip have?

What do you get this time when you cut along the line you have drawn?

You get a bigger twisted loop!

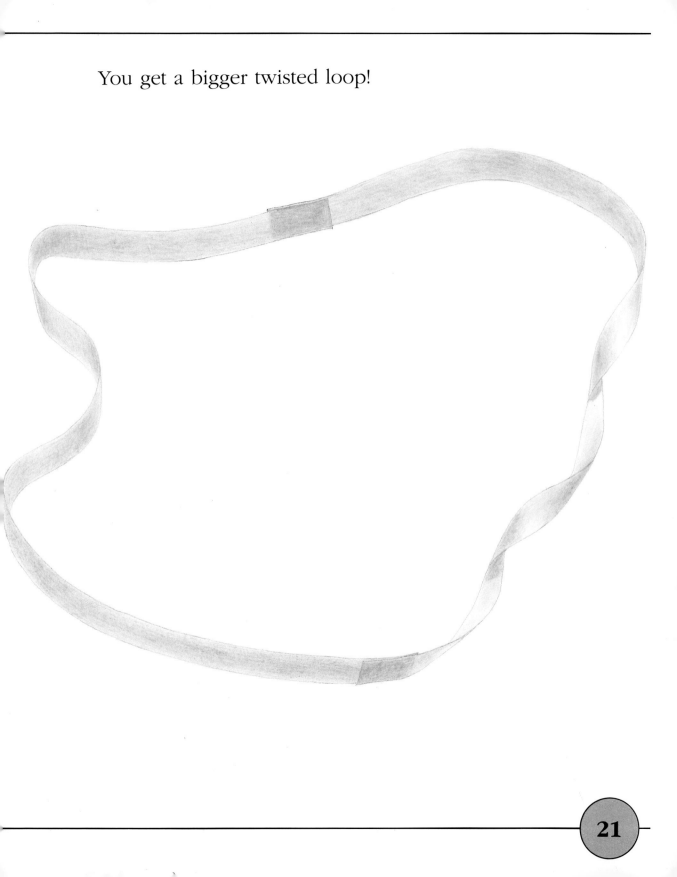

Try a double twist.

Now this time, cut another long strip of paper. Before you tape the ends together to make a loop, twist the strip twice.

Draw a line down the middle of the paper. What happens when you try to draw it back to the starting point?

Cut along the line.
What happens this time?

You get two twisted loops linked together!

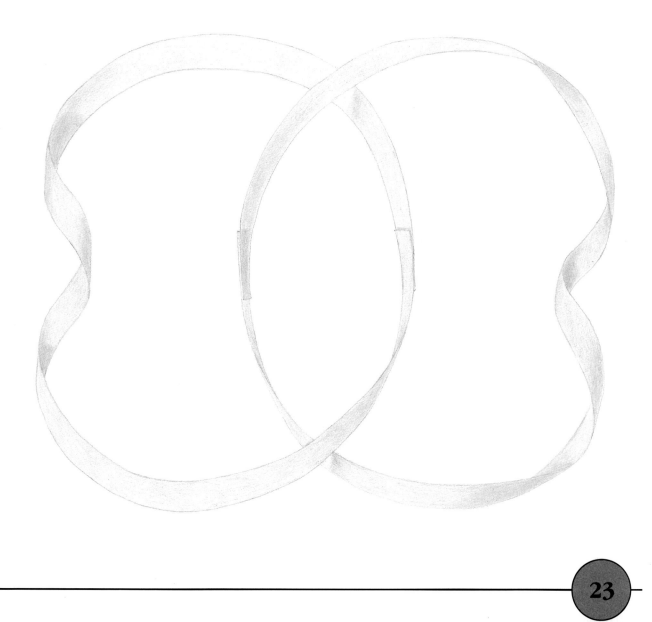

Now, cut a strip of paper and twist it three times. Tape the ends. Draw a line down the middle of the paper. Cut along the line. What happens?

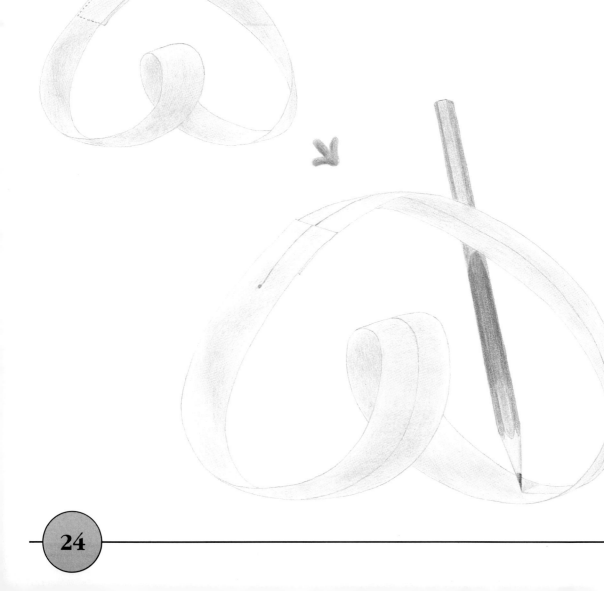

You get a twisted loop!

Try something a little bit harder.

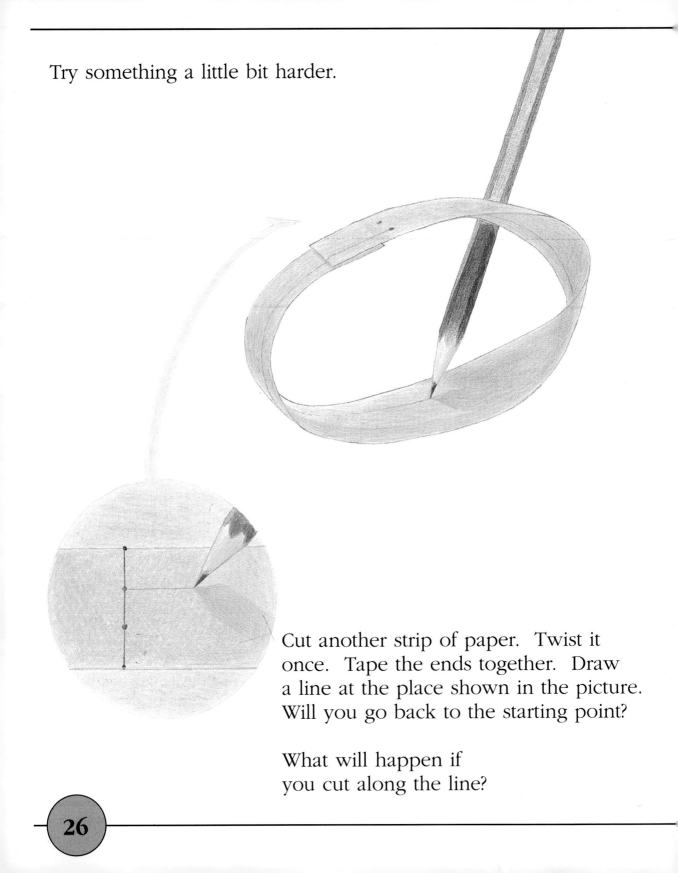

Cut another strip of paper. Twist it
once. Tape the ends together. Draw
a line at the place shown in the picture.
Will you go back to the starting point?

What will happen if
you cut along the line?

You get a twisted large loop and a twisted small loop linked together.

Let's tape two loops together.

A

Cut two long pieces of paper. Draw a line down the middle of both pieces. Make a loop by taping the ends of one piece without twisting it.

Put the other piece of paper through the loop. Tape its ends to make a loop, but don't twist it. Tape the two loops together at the place marked A.

Cut along the line. What happens?

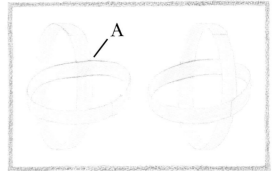

Try taping them in different ways.

This time you get a large square!

How can rings be linked together, but still not linked together?

Look carefully at the drawing below. Is the blue ring linked to the red ring? To the white ring? Is any ring linked to any one other ring?

No, but you still cannot move the rings apart! What is holding the rings together? The next page will help you find out.

Make this puzzle. Cut out three rings. Color one red. Color another one blue. Keep the last one white.

Lay the blue ring on the red one. Cut the white ring apart. Pass the white ring through the blue ring and the red ring. Follow the direction of the arrows in the drawing.

Tape the white ring back together. Now gently try to remove one ring. See how they stay together? Now show others the unexpected things circles can do!

GLOSSARY

Here is a list of words and phrases used in this book. After you read what each word or phrase means, you can see it used in a sentence.

business card: a piece of light cardboard 2 x 3 1/2 inches (5 x 9 cm) printed with the name and address of a business or a person who works for a business
The bookseller gave me his business card so I could write to him.

circle: a shape made by a line that bends evenly until the ends of the line come together
She drew a circle with a red crayon.

clamp: to grip or fasten tightly
Clamp the two pieces of wood together until the glue dries.

container: something that can hold liquids or solids
He put all the apples in containers.

index: something that guides or points something out
The index finger is sometimes called the pointer.

linked: connected or joined together
All the circles were linked into a single chain.

loop: a shape made by a line, a thread, or a piece of string that curves back so the ends touch
He made a loop in the rope.

loop-the-loop: an amusement ride on a metal track that makes a loop that stands upright
He had six rides on the loop-the-loop today.

postcard: a piece of light cardboard 4 x 6 inches (10 x 15 cm) with space for an address on one side and a written message on the other
My aunt and uncle sent me a postcard from Michigan.

ring: a small circular band of metal, plastic, or other material in a rigid shape; a mark in that shape
They played at tossing rings in the yard all afternoon.

surface tension: the tightly stretched surface of water; the tendency of water to round up into drops
The surface tension of the water let the insect run across the pond.

twist: to put a turn in a length of rope, paper, cloth, or other material
He twisted the towel to wring out the water.

INDEX